Lois Wyse

I LOVE YOU BETTER NOW

By Lois Wyse

Poetry

Love Poems for the Very Married
Are You Sure You Love Me?

For Children

Grandmothers Are to Love
Grandfathers Are to Love
Two Guppies, a Turtle, and Aunt Edna
I Wish Every Day Were My Birthday
The Compleat Child (with Joan Javits)
The I Don't Want to Go to Bed Book for Boys
The I Don't Want to Go to Bed Book for Girls

Other Books

P. S. Happy Anniversary
The Absolute Truth About Marriage
What Kind of Girl Are You, Anyway?
Help! I Am the Mother of a Teen-Age Girl

Record Albums

Love Poems for the Very Married (Flying Dutchman)
I Love You Better Now (Flying Dutchman)

I Love you Better Now

Lois Wyse

Garret Press
The World Publishing Company
New York and Cleveland

Published by The Garret Press, 15702 Aldersyde Drive, Cleveland, Ohio 44120. Distributed by The World Publishing Company, 2231 West 110th Street, Cleveland, Ohio 44102. Published simultaneously in Canada by Nelson, Foster & Scott, Ltd. First printing-June, 1970.
Library of Congress Catalog Card Number: 72-115802. Printed in the United States of America.

A Garret Press Book

**Because
I still do.**

Contents

I Love You Better Now   1
Saturday Night   3
Three Weeks in a Cold House   5
Just Because I Look Positive Doesn't Mean I Am Positive   7
Have I Given You a Valentine Lately?   9
Song of Love   11
To Be Perfectly Honest   13
Nobody Is Born Free   15
The Checkup   17
A Thousand Tiny Terrors   19
I'll Meet You at 5 at the Plaza   21
Interplanetary Message   23
The Reality of Reality   25
I Love You Better Now, Part II   27
Do We Have to Go Out Tonight?   29
I'm Fine. Really I Am.   31
Projection   33
Please Tell Me That You Love Me Every Day   35
Turn Once to the Left   37
Reflections on a Birthday   39
Look at Us   41
Call the Weather Lady   43
Nobody Knows You Quite Like This   45
Lesson #437   47
And the Green Grass Grows All Around   49
Postponed on Account of War   51
English Lesson   53
You Don't Have to Love Me Forever   55

I Love You Better Now

Before I was in love with you,
I was in love with love.
Oh, what a lovely love
Of cloudless climes and starry skies
With a man that never was.

> This was me.
> The me who lived with girly girl beliefs
> When first she lived with you
> Until little by little,
> Slice by slice,
> Like the layers of wallpaper
> In a hundred-year-old house
> You stripped the pink dreams down.
>> Off with the cabbage roses.
>> Down with the merry maids.

Backward turns the clock.

Where does reality begin?
When did you peel the last old pattern
And find there really was a woman
Under such a lot of girl?

Saturday Night

It is party time party time party
Time to smile at all the people
Laugh dance eat sing ha ha drink go home
And rewind my tape.

Three Weeks in a Cold House

You were away again.
You are away so often now,
And I walked through the quiet house
Because I never did learn how
To make the time go fast
When you go far from me.
I turned on the stereo
To drown the throbbing of my thoughts
And learned again
It doesn't work
To substitute slick lyrics
For the quiet of your voice.

I looked around the house,
This repository of old books
           new magazines
           a pool table
           paintings
           flowers
           antiques
           crystal
           clocks
           pianos
           lamps
           and one electric typewriter with a ribbon
I can't change.
Before me was the worldly wealth that comes unglued
        each time you go away,
Little loosenings of the love that put it all together.
           Hurry back before Newsweek is out of date.
I think there is a crack in the bottom of the pool.
        Or is it just a fault of love?
Turn up the stereo, somebody.
I still can hear me cry.

Just Because I Look Positive Doesn't Mean I Am Positive

It is two weeks since you have wondered
Where I stood
With us.

But I have wondered longer.

Have I Given You A Valentine Lately?

I don't believe in Valentines.
They are young and vulnerable
And hopelessly old-fashioned.

Valentines are for
Sentimental sentimentalists,
Romantic romantics,
And those who still believe in
Happy endings.

I am at that point in life
When I know how the story ends
And when the nights grow cold.
So I do not expect
Lace slips,
Surprise trips,
Cherry flips,
Or tender little poems
Because it is That Day.

Instead I want my Valentines
At unexpected times.
I want to know you think of me
In mid-May, March, and June.
For I believe,
My dear,
One day a year
Is not enough for love.

Song Of Love

Out of this,
The window of our room,
I see a hundred people
Marching by. A different drummer plays for each.
Oh, my darling, little do they know
That just six stories up
Rat-a-tat-tat
Violins are playing songs of love.
Hurry. One, two.
To the job. Three, four.
I am so glad today I cannot hear
Those distant drums.

To Be Perfectly Honest

Honesty is what the witless
Give each other.
Out of all the possibilities
For life
How very good it is
That we have never made a virtue out of honesty.

For love itself is not an honest thing.
It is instead
A formless something that we shape,
A no-color miracle we paint,
A fancy that we free,
A bridge for two
To span long separations.

And in this created innocence,
In this, the perfect love world that we build,
The adding, dear, of honesty
Would be a most dishonest thing.

Nobody Is Born Free

I was a prisoner of my maidenhood
And kept a tight, taut time
To the rhythm of the world.
I wore blinders on my body
Better to control the life I thought I led.
Yet I said that I was free.

But I was not.
I never knew what freedom was
Until I gave myself to you
And learned that it is love
That sets me free
To live the life I thought I led.

The Checkup

There is the sweet sick smell of health
In this, the doctor's office,
And I await his watchful word.
He smiles his little doctor smile and creaks back in his chair,
"The checkup's fine. You are all right."

But I knew that before.

So why did I endure
The probes and prods of that white-coated man?
Simply to assure myself
It's safe to let you love me.
Love me.
Love me.
Please love me.

A Thousand Tiny Terrors

When a thousand tiny terrors
Lace their icy lines through me
I'll turn to you, my love,
Because I am afraid no more
To say, "I am afraid."

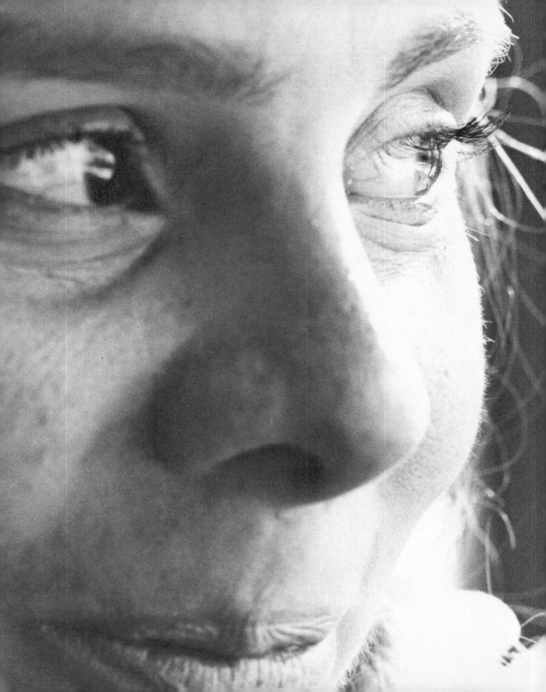

I'll Meet You At 5 At The Plaza

I wait now
In this
Staid and proper room
For the man
Both staid and proper
Who will envelop me
Not with a
Passion-free
Perfunctory
Peck on just my cheek
But with a look.

All the staid and proper people
Will nod and sip their tea.
Not me
I know what that look means.

Interplanetary Message

Three astronauts
Are orbiting the moon
And now we know
The pools and heights of
That strange surface.

But what flights of fancy
Will explore
The cunning craters
Of your mind?

The Reality Of Reality

I would like to tell you the truth,
But I am not sure what I did with it.

I Love You Better Now, Part II

There it was.
>Half a sandwich,
>Lukewarm drink.

The remnants of your lonely lunch.

And as I cleaned
The scrips and scraps
I came across a note you wrote.
A note that was not meant for me.
A scribble of some random thoughts.

And in the margin of the note
I saw my name
Hatched and scratched
In some unconscious half-time.

I put the little paper
In the pocket of my skirt
And each time I touch it
I know well
That I would rather gather
Half your time
And half your thoughts
Than all
Of any other man.

Do We Have to Go Out Tonight?

I can remember
When I loved
Parties.

Very big or very little
It really did not
Matter.

But now I am not party-prone.
I now like people more and things
Less.

I'm Fine. Really I Am.

The coldness of the day is right for me;
It matches all the grey I feel inside.

       Stone
       Concrete
       Ash
       Dust
       Where did all the flowers go?

Do you think that when it's June my fingers will not be so stiff
and cold?
Do you think the sun can melt my hard, bright, brittle shell?

       Do you?
       Do you?
       Do you think?

Projection

On days when everything goes wrong
I say to me,
"One year from now,
And it will all be right."

What will I say
One year from now?

Please Tell Me That You Love Me Every Day

Do not depend on what has gone before
To enchant our life that is to be,
For sometimes I remember the wrong things
And I never was too good at taking memories to bed.

Turn Once to the Left

I am the keeper of my flame,
The mistress of my house.
I alone preside
Over silences and rages.

So let me be.
Stop asking what I want,
For what I want is locked in me.
Let me be.

But do not forget,
That though I lock
My deep and private self,
You hold the only key.

Use it.
Let me be.

Reflections on a Birthday

The thing that makes old age for some
A scary proposition
Is knowing that perhaps one day
The past may
Look much brighter than the future.

But not for me.
Not for me.
So long as I awake each day
With love and you, my dear,
My future's filled with hope,
And I am young.

Look at Us

I introduced a man who needed
To a woman who needs
And they formed
A Necessary Alliance.

Does reliance
Make the best alliance?

Not always.
Look at us.
Very good alliance,
But we are self-reliants.
For example,
I had a marvelous day today,
And I didn't even see you.

But how will
Tough
Strong
Thrifty
Brave
And reverent me
Get through tonight?

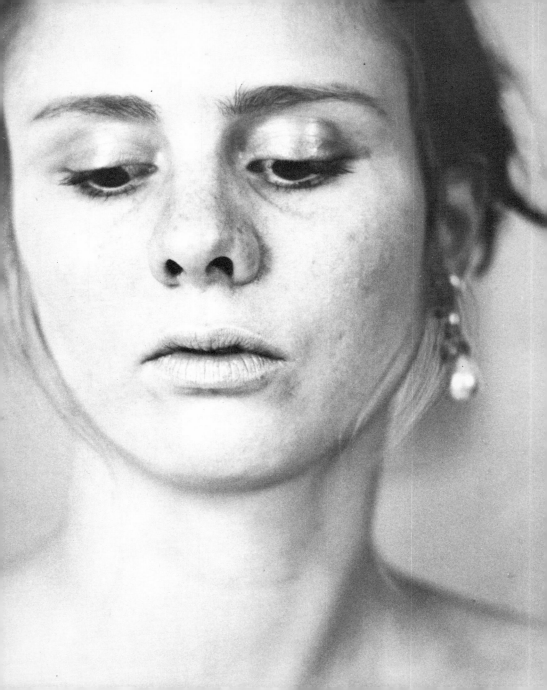

Call the Weather Lady

Hot day.
Hot day.
93.
Hot day.
Bomb.
Cough.
Wilt.
Air condition
The human
State

All
winter long,
even though
The bombs burn longer on a
Hot day.

Nobody Knows You Quite Like This

I think you are
Wise, witty,
Warm and wonderful.

Yet there are those
Who do not find you so.

But if,
Since I have known you,
I have found
Wise and witty
Wonder warmth
Nestled in my heart,
Who is to say
You did not put it there?

From this deep exchange between us
I have learned that our love grows
Not just with what we give
But also with the
When and
Where and
Why
Of just how much we take.

And the Green Grass Grows All Around

I had dinner with a bachelor tonight,
And he was all the things a bachelor should be:
Witty, bright, urbane is he
Who goes to Everywhere in season
And orders out-of-season things
In French.

> Would you trade places, dear, with him?
> I think you might.
> But let me add he, too,
> Might willingly place trade with you.

Yet in a day or two
I think both would return
Each to the life that best he knows.
You see, my dear,
The routines of other men
Look good until they're lived.

> The same is true
> Of women.
> I am so glad
> I'm home.

Postponed On Account Of War

There never was a better time than now.
So why do we assign to some
Bomb-scared, world-scarred future
Our shining hopes and dreams?

English Lesson

It was a lovely day-night
All love all day all night.
I am so full of
What I feel
For you.

Full-feeled.
Filled full.
Fulfilled.
Yes. That's the word.

You Don't Have to Love Me Forever

It is not easy to be married.
It is not a simple thing
To be a part of someone else
When what I really want
Is to find the parts of me.

The diverse parts of me,
The funny sads,
The sad funnies.
I am changing all the time.
I can't keep up with me.
So I don't expect a love that knows no change.
I ask only that you
      Love me here
      Love me now
      Love me warm
But you don't have to love me forever.

I mean that.

You don't have to love me forever.
But wouldn't it be something
If you did?

The Author

Lois Wohlgemuth Wyse was born and raised in Cleveland, is a one-time newspaper reporter (The Cleveland Press) and a full-time advertising executive (Wyse Advertising, corporate creative director). Her articles and poems have appeared in a number of magazines in the United States, Germany, and Australia. At present she is working on a non-fiction book, Mrs. Success, which probes the lives and problems of women married to successful men. Mrs. Wyse is married to Marc A. Wyse (president of Wyse Advertising), and they are the parents of two children, Katherine and Robert.

Designed by Myrna Sebastian

Photographs by Elliott Landy